THE BEST OF MAC 2011

Cartoons from the *Daily Mail*

Stan McMurtry **mac**

Edited by Mark Bryant

PORTICO

For my wonderful grandchildren: Nick, Katie, Megan, Finlay and Tom.
And of course, their equally wonderful parents.

First published in the United Kingdom in 2011 by
Portico Books
10 Southcombe Street
London
W14 0RA

An imprint of Anova Books Company Ltd

ISBN 9781907554377

A CIP catalogue record for this book is available from the British Library.

10 9 8 7 6 5 4 3 2 1

Printed and bound by TJ International, Padstow, UK

This book can be ordered direct from the publisher at www.anovabooks.com

Preface

What a year it's been. Public spending cuts, a Coalition Government burning rubber doing U-turns, a summer of scandals and our brave soldiers still at war in Afghanistan and Libya.

Thank heavens for the royal wedding which brought some cheer to all the bad news. Perhaps this selection of the year's cartoons will also conjure up a smile or two. I hope so.

MAC

For the first time in 20 years the Queen asked for a rise in her Civil List allowance to plug the gap in the royal household's finances. The shortfall of £6 million a year was being met by an emergency reserve due to run out in 2012.

'What does one want? ... A £6 million rise! ... When does one want it? ... Before one's country goes broke!' *1 June 2010*

The Aston Martin DB5 driven by Sean Connery as James Bond in *Goldfinger* (1964) and *Thunderball* (1965) – featuring revolving number plates, a bullet-proof shield, an ejector seat and other gadgets – was put up for auction at £4 million.

'My wife wants to know what the little red button is for.' *3 June*

David Cameron told Britons to prepare themselves for 'years of pain' as he announced that Chancellor George Osborne's forthcoming Budget would include the deepest public spending cuts for decades.

'Ladies and gentlemen, I have some wonderful news …' *8 June*

A 20-year-old Romanian man survived temperatures of -41°C when he stowed away in the undercarriage of a Boeing 747 flying from Vienna to London. Meanwhile, the countdown began for the football World Cup in South Africa.

'It's your mum. You left our match tickets on the mantelpiece at home.' *11 June*

A 33-year-old traffic policeman was sentenced to 3½ years in jail by Cardiff Crown Court for letting women drivers off motoring offences in return for sex.

'Tut, tut, madam. 32 miles an hour! You could lose your licence – but I might be able to help ...' *17 June*

England fans arriving in South Africa for the World Cup in South Africa were quick to adopt the use of the local 140-decibel *vuvuzela* plastic horn.

'I said: "They're useful after a match as well, aren't they?" '18 June

After 183 games and 980 points, 25-year-old John Isner of the USA beat 28-year-old Nicolas Mahut of France at Wimbledon in the longest professional tennis match in history, lasting 11 hours and 5 minutes.

'Can you do anything, doctor? He's just umpired Wimbledon's longest ever tennis match.' *25 June*

Tate Britain's exhibition 'Harrier and Jaguar', by artist Fiona Banner, featured a former Royal Navy Sea Harrier jump-jet suspended nose-down from the ceiling together with an RAF Jaguar fighter that had flown in Operation Desert Storm against Iraq in 1991.

'Yes. Mummy is very cross. I told you not to climb inside or press any buttons!' *30 June*

There was considerable controversy when Justice Secretary Ken Clarke announced in a speech at the Centre for Crime & Justice Studies in London that 'warehousing' convicts was 'ineffectual' and proposed that fewer offenders should be sent to jail.

'Sorry to wake you, Mr Clarke. We couldn't leave without telling you your stance on keeping criminals out of prison has our full support.' *1 July*

The TaxPayers' Alliance attacked a scheme in Birmingham, funded by the NHS, which taught unemployed women at risk from developing mental health problems as a result of loneliness and isolation to create stand-up comedy routines based on their experiences.

'Okay, Mrs Warburton. You're standing up now. Remember, try not to mumble.' *7 July*

A group of elderly residents living in a troubled housing estate in Leicester installed hi-tech surveillance equipment and long-range cameras to trap hooded yobs and drug-dealers plaguing their neighbourhood.

'Keep your eyes open, lads. Some pensioners wiv hidden cameras 'ave been taking sneaky pictures of us to hand to the police.' *8 July*

Former merchant seaman, trade-union leader and Labour Deputy Prime Minister John Prescott, who had once punched a protester, denied that his ennoblement as Lord Prescott of Kingston-upon-Hull was a betrayal of his socialist principles.

'Ah, Reggie, you've just missed a most stimulating discussion with Lord Prescott about the abject betrayal of his socialist principles.' *9 July*

It was revealed that the head teacher of an inner-city primary school in Lewisham, south London, was paid more than £276,000 last year, a salary higher than the head of the prestigious secondary school, Eton College.

'The headmaster is counting his money right now. Would Sir care for a glass of chilled chablis while he waits?' *14 July*

Following the announcement that full-face Islamic veils were to be banned in France, Environment Secretary Caroline Spelman declared that wearing a burka 'empowered' women.

'Doris, love. How would you like to feel empowered?' *20 July*

David Cameron's first ever official talks at the White House with President Obama were marked by a friendly mood reminiscent of his relationship with Deputy Prime Minister Nick Clegg. Meanwhile, back home, Samantha Cameron was due to give birth.

'Goodbye, Dave. And give your partner Clegg my best wishes for the birth.' *22 July*

David Cameron launched a new 'National Citizen Service' involving thousands of 16-year-olds being sent to summer camps for seven weeks at a cost of £1400 each.

'Mum. What were press gangs?' *23 July*

It was revealed that BP's chief executive, Tony Hayward, who had been in charge of the company during the disastrous Gulf of Mexico oil spoil, was to leave with a payoff of more than £1 million and a pension worth £450,000 a year.

'Filthy lucre. Is that the same stuff we're covered in?' *27 July*

Home Secretary Theresa May announced plans to involve more members of the public in the police force, including 50,000 extra special constables and new part-time 'police reservists'.

'Can't stop. I've got a 999 call!' *28 July*

Cabinet Office Minister Francis Maude attacked the large number of civil servants who seemed to do little work but could not be removed because of the huge cost of making them redundant.

'Looks like the cabinet minister's got the problem sorted ... whoops. There goes old Mr Farqueson ...' *29 July*

The Government announced that, from October 2010, workers will no longer be forced to retire at 65, bringing an end to the idea that people are 'past it' when they reach this age.

'Right. That seems to be unanimous. Nobody can remember exactly what it is we do here.' *30 July*

Despite Government plans to cap the number of immigrants allowed into the UK from outside Europe, the Department for Business, Innovation & Skills proposed that more foreign students from these countries would be allowed into the country.

'It's Cameron's promise to put a cap on immigration.' *3 August*

The Food Standards Agency began an investigation when a dairy farmer admitted that milk from the offspring of cloned cows had been supplied illegally to high-street shops without being labelled or identified as such.

'If the penicillin doesn't work try weaning her off the cloned cow's milk.' *4 August*

An article in an Italian newspaper claimed that three women had shared a bed with the country's 73-year-old Prime Minister, Silvio Berlusconi, at a party in his official residence in Rome.

'Can I finish cleaning the room now, Mr Berlusconi?' *5 August*

As supermarkets refused to accept milk from cloned cows it was revealed that meat from cloned cattle had also illegally entered the food chain.

'What's the point of it all? They don't want our milk, they don't want our meat ...' *6 August*

At the trial of the former President of Liberia, Charles Taylor, British model Naomi Campbell admitted she had accepted 'blood diamonds' from the dictator after meeting him at a dinner given by South Africa President Nelson Mandela in Pretoria in 1997.

'Concrete? A lecherous old b****** last night told me it was a blood diamond!' *10 August*

The Government announced that it would declare war on benefits cheats in an attempt to crack down on the estimated £5.2 billion lost each year to fraud and error in the welfare system.

'We have your shopping list, Sunshine! What would someone on incapacity benefits want with athlete's foot cream?' *11 August*

Following earlier demonstrations by protesters against Britain's involvement in the Iraq War, strict security arrangements were planned to protect former Prime Minister Tony Blair at the launch of his autobiography, *A Journey*, at Waterstone's bookshop in London.

'Yes, Mr Blair. Everything's ready for your book signing. We're doing final rehearsals now.' *13 August*

After years of promises by previous governments, Health Secretary Andrew Lansley announced that mixed-sex wards in NHS hospitals would finally be axed by the end of the year.

'At least this government has made a start – I see that woman in the next bed has gone.' *17 August*

Work and Pensions Secretary Iain Duncan Smith revealed plans to axe winter fuel allowances for better-off pensioners. Meanwhile, an official police study reported that the number of cannabis factories in Britain had doubled since last year.

'At first the prospect of losing our winter fuel allowance was a bit of a blow – would you like a spliff with your tea?' *19 August*

Former Prime Minister Gordon Brown was taken on by an international speakers' bureau to give lectures in Asia and the Middle East at the rate of £64,000 per engagement.

'... and now, with the first of his £64,000 speeches. Please give a big hand to your husband – Gordon Brown!' *20 August*

The new series of ITV's popular *The X Factor* talent show was accused of fakery when it was discovered that hi-tech 'auto-tuning' technology had been used to enhance contestants' voices.

'Get ready ... high note coming up ...' *24 August*

There was a public outcry when a middle-aged woman in Coventry was caught on CCTV dumping a four-year-old tabby cat in a wheelie bin.

'I'd better go, Mavis. Somebody's dumped another poor cat in our wheelie bin.' *25 August*

A Hertfordshire man who invented a button-less 'magic wand' remote control which could operate TV, hi-fi, laptops and other electronic devices, received a record £200,000 of investment from the panel of BBC2 TV's *Dragons' Den*.

'George. About that new "wand" remote control you bought ... I think you must have wiggled when you should've waggled.' *26 August*

British police questioned four Pakistani cricketers over allegations of match fixing involving an international betting syndicate during the final Test between Pakistan and England.

'I have a horrid feeling Mrs Frobisher has been got at by an Asian betting syndicate ...' *31 August*

There was a storm of protest when Defence Secretary Liam Fox announced that he was in talks with the French government over plans for the two countries to share Royal Navy aircraft carriers.

'I think he jumped!' *1 September*

In a dramatic result, former Foreign Secretary David Miliband was narrowly beaten by his younger brother Ed in the Labour Party leadership contest.

'I'm sorry. I didn't want my political ambitions thwarted, so I sold him on eBay.' *28 September*

A report by the Financial Services Authority revealed that British banks received more than 7000 complaints a day about sloppy service and poor advice. Meanwhile, Prince Charles opened the Ryder Cup golf tournament at Celtic Manor, Newport, Wales.

'What is it this time, Mrs Warburton? Yesterday it was complaints about sloppy service!' *1 October*

At the Conservative Party's annual conference in Birmingham Chancellor George Osborne defended his robust programme of cuts that included the ending of child benefits and tax credits to middle-class families earning more than £50,000 a year.

'Y'know, Henrietta, I have a horrid feeling that that bounder Osborne has stopped Ma and Pa's child benefits.' *5 October*

A Government shake-up in university funding removed the cap on tuition fees, sending the costs of undergraduate student courses at Oxford, Cambridge and other top academic institutions soaring to £12,000 a year.

'Look, Simon. Mummy and Daddy have bought you a hoodie – why not bunk off school and join a nice gang of yobs?' *12 October*

After 68 days, the first of 33 men trapped half a mile underground after a tunnel collapsed in the San José mine in Chile was rescued using a specially designed escape pod.

'Someone's in trouble when he comes up – he forgot their wedding anniversary.' *13 October*

Justice Secretary Ken Clarke declared that he wanted to reduce sharply the number of short-term prison sentences, leading to fears that those guilty of grievous bodily harm and other violent offences would remain on the streets.

'Shan't be long. I'm just popping out to beat the c**p out of Ken Clarke.' *15 October*

64-year-old actress Felicity Kendal, best known for her role in TV's *The Good Life*, did the splits during a raunchy rumba routine with her 31-year-old dance partner Vincent Simone on the BBC's *Strictly Come Dancing*.

'She's been watching Felicity Kendal on *Strictly Come Dancing*.' *19 October*

As prisoners faced the prospect of early release from jail the outside world seemed less inviting. As well as economic hardships Britons faced the increased threat of terrorism, including cyber attacks capable of causing airliners to fall from the sky.

'It's no use you crying and pleading, Higgins. You're being released early!' *20 October*

In his 'Emergency Budget' Chancellor George Osborne announced that £18.5 billion a year would be slashed from benefits spending. However, those over 60 would still retain their winter fuel allowance and free bus passes and eye tests.

'Wonderful news, Gerald. When we go back to the UK each spring our winter fuel allowance will still be waiting for us.' *21 October*

The Queen was not spared in the Government's expenditure cuts and was informed that the royal budget would fall by 14% over the next three years. Meanwhile, Manchester United striker Wayne Rooney agreed a new pay deal with the club for £10.4 million a year.

'We're saved! I've asked Wayne Rooney for a loan.' *22 October*

Internet search giant Google admitted it had 'mistakenly collected' millions of passwords and private emails from home computers during its Street View project in which almost every road in Britain had been photographed using its special vehicles.

'Mummy, Daddy. There's a man from Google in a van outside who's seen my bank account and wants to marry me!' *26 October*

The Fire Brigades' Union threatened to stage a walkout on 5 November, Bonfire Night, in a protest over plans to re-employ 5000 firemen on new shift patterns.

'Right, lads. Somebody nip downstairs and set off the alarm.' *27 October*

The sudden disappearance of the Emperor of Exmoor, a 12-year-old, nine-feet-tall, 22-stone red deer stag – believed to be Britain's largest wild animal – led to suspicions that it had been shot by trophy-hunters.

' ... and why Exmoor? They've got perfectly good hat-stands down the road at Ikea!' *28 October*

In his first public speech as head of MI6, spy chief Sir John Sawers condemned the use of torture as 'illegal and abhorrent' but admitted that, though outlawed in the UK, Britain's intelligence service did use information gained by this means from other countries.

'Stop moaning, Farqueson. You'll stay up there till you admit slipping laxatives into M's tea!' *29 October*

In the run-up to Guy Fawkes Night a 'dummy bomb' made from a toner ink cartridge caused a major terrorist alert when it was discovered at East Midlands airport on a plane from Yemen bound for Chicago.

'Freeze! And drop the matches! We have reason to believe you are in possession of small tubes of cardboard packed with explosives!' *2 November*

The Prime Minister's personal photographer, and later the producer of his pre-election 'WebCameron' videos, became civil servants in the Cabinet Office.

'Relax, Samantha. He's on the payroll now.' *5 November*

63-year-old former MP Ann Widdecombe appeared on TV's *Strictly Come Dancing*.
Her hilarious attempt at the Charleston received the lowest score from the judges
but audience reaction got her through to the next round of the competition.

'No, no, no! We want bums on seats, love ... Can't you move a little more like Ann Widdecombe?' *9 November*

In his autobiography, *Decision Points*, former US President George W. Bush defended the controversial use of 'waterboarding', a simulated drowning technique used by US soldiers while interrogating Al Qaeda suspects.

'Y'know, cook. Mr Bush is right. There was too much salt in the potatoes.' *10 November*

In the most far-reaching welfare reforms for decades, Work & Pensions Secretary Iain Duncan Smith unveiled a new package which included plans to strip benefits for up to three years from claimants who refuse to take jobs.

'We don't want to be here any more than you, mate. But it's a case of get a job or no benefits.' *12 November*

Prime Minister David Cameron announced that he had asked the Office for National Statistics to devise a questionnaire to measure how happy or sad people are in the UK.

'So in general, sir, would you say you were happy, unhappy or just a little bit depressed?' *16 November*

Nine years after they met as students at the University of St Andrews, Prince William and Kate Middleton officially announced their engagement. Speculation mounted as to whether the wedding would be at Westminster Abbey or St Paul's Cathedral.

'You're right, madam. The pavements will be packed. But trust me, not for a good while yet.' *17 November*

A BBC *Panorama* investigation revealed that children as young as six were being taught Islamic Sharia law at a network of Muslim weekend schools across the UK. Sharia law's punishments include cutting off a criminal's hand for theft.

' ... and this line tells me you stole 50p from your daughter's piggy bank.' *23 November*

As plans for the marriage of Prince William and Kate Middleton began to take shape it was announced that it was to be a 'People's Royal Wedding' and invitations would be sent out to scores of ordinary citizens.

'... and remember it's morning suits with top hats and here's a Harrods wedding present suggestion list.' *25 November*

During the protests in London against university tuition fees, rioting schoolgirls joined a mob which attacked a police squad van, smashed its windows, daubed its sides with graffiti and looted police uniforms and helmets.

'Lucinda, dear. On your way home from school on Wednesday did you happen to see a policeman's helmet?' *26 November*

New disclosures from classified US diplomatic cables published by whistle-blowing website
WikiLeaks caused considerable international embarrassment. Meanwhile, Britain suffered
its heaviest snowfall since 1993 with worse predicted.

'I wish you'd turn that radio off. Every time they mention WikiLeaks, Grandad has to go.' *1 December*

As 10-foot drifts were reported in Scotland, a total whiteout spread across the rest of Britain with the east coast of England suffering badly.

'Was it my imagination or did I hear the first carol singers last night?' *2 December*

As the WikiLeaks revelations continued, a 64-year-old Liberal Democrat MP hit the headlines when his 25-year-old female research assistant, who had access to official documents on UK defence policy, was suspected of being a Russian spy.

'It's all right. She's not a Russian spy. She's a researcher for a company called WikiLeaks.' *7 December*

During another protest in London by students and lecturers against tuition fees, police were criticised for their use of the controversial 'kettling' technique, completely surrounding demonstrators and not releasing them for hours.

'Sorry I'm late home, darling. I've been kettled by the police.' *10 December*

As angry students converged on London for fresh protests over university tuition fees, police ruled out the use of water cannon, despite the fact that the limousine carrying Prince Charles and the Duchess of Cornwall had been attacked on a previous occasion.

'Gift-wrap it please, Benskin. I don't want Camilla to see her Christmas present too early.' *14 December*

Thousands of viewers complained about lewd performances by US pop stars Christina Aguilera and Rihanna on ITV's *The X Factor*, which seemed to break the broadcasting code of what was suitable to screen on a family show.

'Yeah. Three days ago. Right in the middle of *The X Factor* he suddenly decided to have a cold bath.' *15 December*

As fresh heavy snowfalls on the west of England added to the chaos it was revealed that millions of Christmas gifts bought via the internet were held up in warehouses across the country because weather conditions made deliveries impossible.

'... and don't give me that old codswallop about online presents being delayed 'cos of snow and ice – that's why you've got a flippin' sledge!' *17 December*

As the big freeze set in thousands of Christmas holidaymakers were stranded at Heathrow airport and the grit supply for the nation's roads was also soon in short supply.

'Cooee! Prepare for take-off – we've brought some grit.' *21 December*

After repeated flight cancellations, Heathrow's terminal buildings began to resemble a Third World refugee camp. Meanwhile, naturalists claimed that listening to recordings of birdsong for five minutes each day could help beat the winter blues.

'All together now ... "I'm Dreaming of a White Christmas ..." ' *22 December*

Figures published by the NHS Information Centre revealed that the number of people in England admitted to hospital because they are dangerously overweight had soared almost tenfold in the past five years with more than three-quarters of the patients being women.

'Yeah. We solved that problem. Instead of a turkey this year, we had Wayne's mum.' *29 December*

63-year-old pop singer Sir Elton John and his civil partner David Furnish announced the birth of their surrogate son, Zachary Jackson Levon Furnish-John, who had been born on Christmas Day.

'We may have to take the tree down, Elton. Google says they need feeding from time to time.' *30 December*

Official Department of Work & Pensions figures revealed that, as a result of improved diets and living conditions, as well as advances in medical technology, one in six of the population of Britain could now expect to live to be 100 years old.

'My New Year's resolution is to take up golf and to be that one person in six. What's yours, fatso?' *31 December*

The severe weather over the Christmas period was blamed by local councils for a nationwide household waste mountain with dustmen in some areas being unable to collect rubbish for almost a month because of the heavy snow and ice.

'What a Christmas and start to the New Year, eh? I think we should leave the dustmen a tip.' *4 January 2011*

As the price of gold soared, high-street supermarket chain Tesco began a trial of a new online and instore pawnbroking service, Tesco's Gold Exchange, offering cash for unwanted jewellery, watches, bracelets, rings and other valuables.

'You stingy old git! She says your watch I just nicked is rubbish!' *5 January*

A 64-year-old motorist was fined at Grimsby Magistrates Court for flashing his headlights at oncoming vehicles to warn them of a police speed trap ahead.

'Slow down! Perhaps he's flashing to warn us of a speed trap ahead.' *6 January*

There was public anger when it was revealed that senior executives at major banks, some of which had only recently been bailed out with taxpayers' money, were planning to accept huge annual bonuses.

'Don't trust his sort, Winifred! Bankers suck the blood out of you then expect a big bonus.' *11 January*

The Chinese government donated a breeding pair of giant pandas, Tian Tian and Yangguang, to Edinburgh Zoo. Meanwhile, allegations were made by a former employee at Knowsley Safari Park, near Liverpool, about the inhumane culling of its surplus stock.

'They must've heard that they're going to be sent to Britain.' *12 January*

In a landmark ruling over ageism at the BBC, former *Countryfile* presenter Miriam O'Reilly, axed at the age of 51, won her case at an employment tribunal. Meanwhile, thousands were made homeless by floods in Queensland, Australia.

'Not only are there terrible floods in Australia but I've had to take my cat to the vet and I think I've left my teeth in the ladies' loo.' *13 January*

The owners of a Christian hotel near Penzance, Cornwall, which was also their home, were ordered by a Bristol court to pay compensation to a gay couple whose booking they had refused on religious grounds.

'Isn't that romantic, George, dear? Mr and Mr Smith would like the bridal suite.' *19 January*

Health Secretary Andrew Lansley announced radical changes to the National Health Service, which included the abolition of primary care trusts run by managers and giving the power to spend NHS money to GPs.

'Don't forget to curtsy. All this new power has gone to his head a bit.' *20 January*

In an attempt to save up to £1 billion a year and allow GPs to devote their attention to the most seriously ill, patients were asked to examine themselves at home and then email their symptoms to their doctors rather than meeting them face to face.

'Has the doctor replied to your email yet?' *25 January*

Two male broadcasters for Sky Sports were suspended and later sacked for making sexist remarks about a female line judge during a football match between Wolverhampton Wanderers and Liverpool.

'You're an excellent line judge, Sharon. But I do think you leave yourself open to sexist remarks.' *26 January*

British actor Colin Firth was nominated for (and later won) an Oscar for playing George VI in *The King's Speech*, a film about the king's battle to overcome his stammer. Meanwhile, Mervyn King, Governor of the Bank of England, made gloomy predictions about the future of Britain's economy.

KING'S SPEECH *27 January*

Civil unrest broke out in Egypt in an attempt to topple the oppressive regime of President Hosni Mubarak. As gun battles raged in the streets an estimated 30,000 British tourists were stranded in Cairo.

'Psst, Donald. When it's safe to go out, have you got the plane tickets?' *1 February*

As new statistics revealed that four anti-social behaviour incidents are reported to the police every minute, the Home Office launched a new website that allows residents to type in their postcode to see the full extent of crime in their area.

'Well, that's reassuring, Mavis – our street doesn't get a mention.' *2 February*

The Government prepared for a showdown with the European Court of Human Rights in Strasbourg when it ruled that convicted prisoners in Britain should have the right to vote in parliamentary elections.

'The first thing I'll do if we get the vote is to get rid of that Harold Wilson.' *3 February*

It was announced that the Duchess of Cornwall would have a cameo role in BBC Radio 4's countryside soap opera *The Archers*, the world's longest-running broadcast drama, which celebrates its 60th anniversary this year.

'Oo arrr, m'dear. Oi've bin doin' a bit o' muck spreadin' back 'ome at 'Ighgrove an' oi'm desperate for a pint down at The Bull.' *4 February*

Prince Andrew came under increasing pressure to resign as Britain's trade ambassador after it was discovered that he had links with a disgraced billionaire involved in a sex scandal who had also helped pay off some of the Duchess of York's debts.

'Be honest with me, Philip. Are you going after grouse, pheasant or Andrew?' *8 March*

When Home Secretary Theresa May proposed radical cuts to police pay, perks and overtime, the Police Federation threatened industrial action, including the possibility of a massive march through the streets of London.

''Ello, 'ello, 'ello!' *10 March*

After London Olympics chief Lord Coe launched the official sales website for the games, there was a race to apply for the 6.5 million tickets available, ranging from £20 to £2012 each depending on the sport, date and seat.

'After all our efforts, I've heard a nasty rumour we may have to buy tickets.' *15 March*

A technical error with the Olympics ticketing system led to 10 million bankcards being rejected as invalid. Meanwhile, a court in Rome heard allegations that Italian Prime Minister Silvio Berlusconi had invited young women to 'bunga bunga' sex parties at his house.

'There must have been another technical glitch – we've been allocated two tickets to a Berlusconi bunga bunga party.' *17 March*

With the growing crisis in Libya and the imposition of a no-fly zone over the country to protect anti-Gaddafi protesters, there were calls to reconsider Britain's recent defence cuts such as the decommissioning of the aircraft carrier HMS *Ark Royal* and its Harrier jump-jets.

'Hang on! It's the Prime Minister. Can we put it all back together again?' *18 March*

As RAF Tornado jets launched raids on Libyan government radar stations, anti-aircraft batteries and supply lines, Defence Secretary Liam Fox said he would consider sanctioning a 'bunker buster' attack on Gaddafi's base if civilian casualties could be avoided.

'I suppose this means I won't be getting an invitation to the royal wedding.' *22 March*

Chancellor George Osborne's Budget included increases in National Insurance and a new squeeze on the middle classes at a time when inflation had reached a 20-year record high. Meanwhile, the conflict in Libya grew increasingly bitter.

'Arthur thinks we should string up tyrants who inflict suffering on their own people.' *23 March*

A welcome Budget announcement was that an additional £100 million would be given to local councils to deal with potholes in Britain's crumbling roads damaged by the severe winter weather.

'Nice job? My husband and the Cortina are still down there!' *24 March*

It was revealed that Prince Harry would spend five days with a team of wounded servicemen who were trekking 200 miles to the North Pole to raise money for the Walking With the Wounded charity of which he is patron.

'Get ready, girls. Prince Harry's nearly here. Let's make this the sexiest show ever.' *30 March*

A new biography of Prince William's fiancée, Kate Middleton, claimed that she had left Downe House public school near Newbury, Berkshire, after only two terms because of bullying by other pupils.

'You went to school with Kate Middleton, dear. Did you see any sign of bullying?' *5 April*

Anne, an abused 59-year-old Asian circus elephant whose plight had been revealed in secret video footage by an animal rights group, found a new home in Longleat Safari Park, Wiltshire.

'I wish she'd go somewhere else with her old circus tricks – I'm suddenly feeling quite inadequate.' *6 April*

Deputy Prime Minister Nick Clegg was accused of hypocrisy when he criticised unpaid internships for the 'sharp-elbowed and well connected'. Meanwhile, local authorities in Somerset began charging the public £2 for using council recycling centres.

'Must be Tories. They reckon it's two quid well spent.' *7 April*

Despite Government promises to reinstate weekly rubbish collections, a survey of 117 local councils revealed that 59% had switched to fortnightly collections.

'Go get your rubbish. It's the home of the councillor in charge of fortnightly collections.' *12 April*

As complaints against nurses reached a record high, the President of the Royal College of Nursing told the RCN's annual conference in Liverpool that some nurses did not deliver 'good care' and were giving the profession a bad name.

'Before you eat my breakfast, read the story about some nurses not being up to the job.' *13 April*

51-year-old 'domestic goddess' Nigella Lawson, who was in Australia to film a new cookery series, was photographed on Bondi beach wearing a baseball cap under the hood of a swimsuit which covered most of her body.

'I told you it would be worth the travelling. That Nigella Lawson is soooo sexy!' *20 April*

A report by the Automobile Association revealed that premiums for fully comprehen[sive] insurance on an average car would soon break the £1000-a-year barrier as a result o[f an] increase in 'cash for crash' faked accidents and other fact[ors]

'Don't look so worried. We've just spent £1000 on car insurance.' *14 April*

In a new twist in the secrecy laws regarding celebrities involved in sex scandals, three appeal court judges ruled that, in order to protect his family, a married man in the entertainment industry who had had an affair could not be named.

'Agreed then? I'll keep your name secret if you keep mine.' *21 April*

In yet another celebrity 'gagging order', a television star was granted a new form of super-injunction suppressing for ever the publication of intimate photos of him with a woman which could have an 'adverse impact' on the health and well-being of his family.

'I'm sorry, Mother. I can't tell you why I'm upset with George – he's got himself a super-injunction gagging order!' *22 April*

51-year-old BBC broadcaster Andrew Marr became the first public figure to voluntarily drop a High Court injunction suppressing reports of his infidelity.

'Yes, I know this will hurt my mistresses and their children, but I'm following Andrew Marr's example and dropping my gagging order...' *27 April*

In the run-up to the royal wedding there was much media discussion about who would be invited. Notable omissions from the guest list were former Labour Prime Ministers Tony Blair and Gordon Brown.

'Don't forget, Gordon. Tomorrow you are Fatima, wife number six of Prince Mohammed of Saudi Arabia.' *28 April*

Around the world millions watched the wedding of Prince William and Kate Middleton at Westminster Abbey. Meanwhile, in the World Snooker Championship at the Crucible in Sheffield, John Higgins beat Ronnie O'Sullivan in a tense quarter-finals match.

'Would anyone mind if I switched over to the snooker?' *29 April*

Al Qaeda leader Osama Bin Laden was shot dead by US Navy Seals in a raid on his home in Abbottabad, Pakistan.

'Is this paradise where I get my 72 virgins and a palace?' *3 May*

As the Pakistani government expressed total surprise that Bin Laden had lived openly for six years in the middle of a town only an hour's drive from the capital, Islamabad, US sources revealed that they had discovered his whereabouts after a tip-off.

'Be honest, Abu – did you tip the Americans off where Bin Laden was hiding?' *4 May*

In the first ever referendum on electoral reform, the public were asked to vote on keeping the traditional 'first past the post' system or changing to a new transferable-vote alternative. In the event 70% opted to keep the current system.

'He was on his way to vote first past the post but didn't make it past the pub.' *6 May*

62-year-old Dominique Strauss-Kahn, head of the International Monetary Fund and the favourite to become the next President of France, was charged with a sex attack on a 32-year-old maid in his luxury suite at the Hotel Sofitel in New York.

'Okay, buster. I'm coming in to clean the room so don't try any funny stuff.' *17 May*

Energy Secretary Chris Huhne faced charges of attempting to pervert the course of justice when his estranged wife claimed that he had asked her to put on her driving licence the penalty points incurred for a speeding offence he had committed.

'He's just popped the question – will I put his penalty points on to my driving licence?' *18 May*

Astonished commuters watched as a man led a white mountain pony onto the platform at Wrexham railway station in North Wales, and then attempted to take it on board a train to Holyhead.

'Just curious. Why the bucket, the shovel and the umbrella?' *20 May*

The striking pink silk 'pretzel' headpiece worn by Princess Beatrice at the royal wedding was sold for £81,000 at a charity auction. Meanwhile, US President Barack Obama and his wife Michelle arrived in London for their first state visit to the UK.

'Smile, honey. We'll be meeting the Queen and that hat cost a lot of money.' *24 May*

As David Cameron and President Obama began their talks in London, Manchester United footballer Ryan Giggs was finally named in a celebrity sex scandal and Hollywood film star Arnold Schwarzenegger admitted fathering a child with his housekeeper.

'Okay. Enough about Ryan Giggs. What's the latest on Arnold Schwarzenegger?' *25 May*

When the Grimsvotn volcano erupted in bankrupt Iceland there were fears that Britain's airports would be closed by the resulting ashcloud, as they had been for a similar eruption last year.

'Okay, we've turned it down a bit. But if there's any more talk about us repaying our debts ... !' *26 May*

A damning report by the Care Quality Commission on pensioner care in NHS wards revealed that three out of 12 NHS trusts visited in the past three months were failing to meet the most basic standards required by law.

27 May

A 33-year-old burglar from Nottingham, who had been sentenced to eight months in prison, was released after serving one month when an appeal court judged that under Article 8 of the Human Rights Act he should be allowed home to look after his five children.

'Think about his human rights, dear. If I put him in prison who's going to look after his poor children?' *31 May*

Justice Secretary Ken Clarke approved a prisoner's request to father a child by artificial insemination while in jail as this was in accordance with his 'right to family life' under Article 8 of the Human Rights Act.

'Yes, darlin'. I got your package and I hope to be doin' the business real soon ... ' *2 June*

25-year-old England and Manchester United striker, Wayne Rooney, announced on Twitter that he had had a hair transplant. The operation involved extracting follicles from the back of the head and implanting them at the front.

'Yes. They take the follicles from the back of your head. But I didn't have any.' *8 June*

The Duke of Edinburgh celebrated his 90th birthday.

'And just think, Philip dear. Only another ten years and you'll be getting a telegram from me.' *10 June*

Work & Pensions Secretary Iain Duncan Smith introduced changes to the State pension age for women. Currently 60, it would initially be raised to 62 and then, in 2018, to 65 (the same age as for men).

'Speaking personally, I don't think the Government should force women to work past 60.' *22 June*

New allegations that journalists at the *News of the World*, owned by Rupert Murdoch, had authorised illegal hacking into the mobile phones of celebrities, royalty and the victims of crime led to the sacking of a number of senior staff and an official police inquiry.

'We're not fired yet, but I've just hacked into Rupert Murcoch's phone and we're about to be.' *7 July*

Irreparably damaged by the phone-hacking scandal, the *News of the World*, Britain's largest circulation newspaper, finally closed after 168 years. Its last issue was published on 10 July 2011.